Anytime
Prayers

Anytime Prayers

Madeleine L'Engle

PHOTOS BY MARIA ROONEY

Harold Shaw Publishers
Wheaton, Illinois

Text copyright © Crosswicks, 1994

Photographs copyright © Maria Rooney, 1994

ISBN 0-87788-055-7

Back cover photo ©1994 by John Rooney

Art and design by David LaPlaca

Library of Congress Cataloging-in-Publication Data

L'Engle, Madeleine.
    Anytime prayers \ by Madeleine L'Engle ; photos by Maria Rooney.
        p. cm.
    ISBN 0-87788-055-7
    1. Children—Prayer-books and devotions—English. [1. Prayer books and devotions.] I. Rooney, Maria, ill. II. Title.
    III. Title: Anytime prayers.
    BV4870.L24 1994
    242'.82—dc20   93-46429
                                                               CIP
                                                                AC

---

99   98   97   96   95   94

10   9   8   7   6   5   4   3   2

Prayers of Creation

Madeleine L'Engle and Maria Rooney dedicate this book to

Josephine, Alan, Bion and Laurie; to John; and to the next generation:

Léna, Charlotte, Edward, Bryson, and Alexander . . .

with love.

In the beginning God created the heavens and the earth.

God called the light "day," and the darkness he called "night." God called the expanse "sky." God called the dry ground "land," and the gathered waters he called "seas." Then God said, "Let the land produce vegetation." God made two great lights—the greater light to govern the day and the lesser light to govern the night. He also made the stars. God said, "Let the water teem with living creatures, and let birds fly above the earth across the expanse of the sky. Let the land produce living creatures according to their kinds. Let us make man in our image, in our likeness."

from Genesis 1

Thank you, God
for making water,
that water over which
your Spirit moved
in the very beginning.
Thank you, God, for making
from the darkness
which was upon the face of the deep
all the wonders which you have made!

And out of the flaming, fiery stars
came our very own star
our sun,
and around our sun you gathered your planets
and on our planet you made water
and land
and all the wondrous green and growing things.
Oh, God, you made it all
and said that it was good.
Thank you, God, for the third day!

Thank you, God, for the sun
by which we see
and by which things grow
And for the moon which pulls the tides
And thank you for the stars
which teach us to sing your praises
in their heavenly harmonies
And show us how to move in your dance
in beauteous pattern
and help us rejoice in all
that
on the fourth day
you did make!

And thank you, God,
for whales and their great song
and seals who so love to play
and fish both great and small
to swim the seven seas
and birds to fly across the sky
and make the fifth day full of joy.

Sea and sky
and birds and fish
and trees and flowers
and then, O Lord, you made
lions and lambs, tigers and titmice,
cows and sparrows,
bears and butterflies,
O Lord, you made a lot on the sixth day
and you weren't finished yet
because then you created us,
your children,
in your own image you created
us.

Alleluia!

In the beginning was the Word
shouting all things into Being
joyfully creating.
And then, dear Lord
you rested,
and showed us how to rest.
Sometimes in the summer
I lie on my back on the grass
and look up through the green leaves
of the apple tree
to the blue of the sky,
and I know that I am,
and I rest.
Is it like that for you?

Special
Times with
God

I will praise you, O LORD, with all my heart; I will tell of all your wonders. I will be glad and rejoice in you; I will sing praise to your name, O Most High. *Psalm 9:1-2*

Oh, come let us sing unto the Lord!
That's what I learned today.
Whenever I sing a new song
for my mother or my father or my teacher,
for my brothers and sisters and friends,
or just for myself because I am happy,
I am really singing for you, God.
Oh, come let us sing unto the Lord!

Lord God,
you took great big handfuls of
chaos and made galaxies
and stars and solar systems
and night and day and sun and rain and snow
and me.
I take paint and crayon and paper
and make worlds, too,
along with you.
It's fun.
Thank you.

Today
we walked in the woods
in the snow
and the trees were dark
and their branches were bare.
I put my arms around a tree
and I leaned against the trunk
and put my ear against the bark
and listened
and I could hear the tree, inside,
living,
waiting,
for the time when God
will bring it back to green.
Do you do that for us, too,
Lord, when we grow old and bare?

Dear Lord
when I am grown
will I get married
and have children
like my mother?
Will I want to be a teacher
or a doctor
or dance on my toes up on a stage?
Will I sing in an opera house?
Will I be the cook in a big restaurant?
Will I do any of these things
and maybe have children, too?
Will you help me
to know who you want me to be
when I grow up?
Will you help me want to be
what you want me to be?

Today it rained
and then while drops still fell
the sun came out
and a rainbow arched across the sky.
Thank you, Lord, for rainbows
that remind us of your promise,
your covenant with your people.
You never break your promise, Lord.
Thank you.

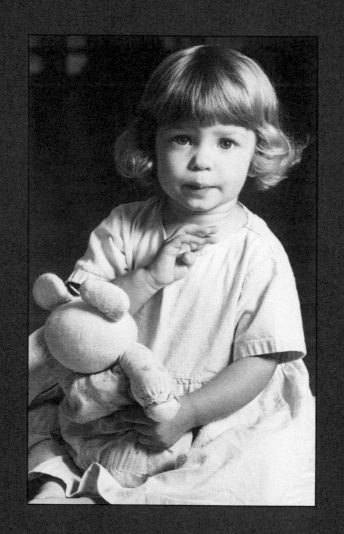

Dear Lord, at night
I go into a new and different world.
I swim through the ocean of sleep
into the strange, bright world of dreams.
I have all kinds of adventures
in all kinds of places
I could never see by day.
Whether I'm waking or dreaming,
you are with me, Lord,
to share in everything that happens.
Thank you for never forgetting me
and for always being with me
and caring.
Amen.

When Bad Things Happen

Thank you, God,
for creating the heavens
with all their glory.
Oh! all the hydrogen clouds
and exploding gasses
and the very firmament of heaven,
your own Creation.
It was your second day!
What joy!

Thank you, God,
for making light,
day and night,
play and sleep,
work and rest.
Night and day became
Your very first day.
How wonderful!
Thank you, Lord.

We know that in all things God works for the good of those who love him, who have been called according to his purpose.

Romans 8:28

Dear God, I'm sorry.
I broke my sister's music box
by winding it too tight.
I didn't mean to, but I did it.
She yelled at me,
so then I yelled at her,
and I wasn't sorry at all.
But now, Lord, that I've said
"I'm sorry," to you,
I can say it to her, too.

Oh, Abba God,
Father, Daddy,
do you know who I am
and why I am sometimes angry?

My friend took my puzzle
and he lost a piece.
He didn't say he was sorry
and he didn't try to find the piece.
I was angry.

My teacher said I should be generous
and forgiving,
and when he turned his back
I stuck out my tongue at him.

Do I love my friend
when I am angry?
When I do not love my friend
can I still love you?

Dear Lord,
Last week
he rode his bike home from school
and the front wheel hit a rock,
and he fell and his head too hit a rock.
He did not stand up again
and he did not cry
and he did not move.
I do not understand
how he could be, last week,
and this week not be.
Be dead.
What does dead mean, Lord?
All I know
is that you love your children
and that you are a good father,
because Jesus said so.
So I know
that a good father
cares for his children
always
and even if I do not know
where my friend is now,
and what he is doing,
you know.
I talked to my mother,
and she said, Yes, that is right.
And if God knows, she said,
then that is all we need.

Yesterday my great-aunt Nanny died.
She was old, and my parents said,
"It's a blessing. She just died in her sleep."
They thanked God for her death and wept.
I did not thank God. I did not weep.
We went to church and we gave her back to God.
We said good prayers and sang a hymn
and still I did not cry.
They thought
I was not old enough to understand
or care.
But when I went to bed and Tig, my dog,
came in and licked my face when the lights were out,
oh, then I cried, and knew, and cared.
Be good to great-aunt Nanny, please, dear God.

For Good Things in Life

I'm sorry.
Why, Lord, is that so hard to say?
First I said: It's not my fault.
Then I said: My friend made me.
I was angry all afternoon
with my friend, with everybody,
with myself.
Then I said: I'm sorry.
Now I'm happy with everybody,
with myself,
and with you, Lord.
Amen.

When you were a child, Lord,
you played with your friends.
Sometimes my friends and I disagree.
Sometimes we fight.
If I make people laugh instead of cry
then you will be happy. And so will I.

He has made everything beautiful in its time.

Ecclesiastes 3:11

It's been a good day!
I praise you, Lord.
I praise you for a ball that bounces high.
I praise you for the friend who runs with me.
I praise you for clothes to keep me warm.
I praise you that I have been free to play,
and now I'm going home.
Alleluia!

Thank you, Lord,
for fairytale creatures
that you have made for our pleasure
and because there is nothing made
that you have not made,
and nothing thought of
that you have not thought of.
Thank you for the seven dwarves
who loved Snow White
and for fairies who sleep
in the bells of flowers
and for elves
who sleep under toadstools
and turn their poison to good bread.
Help us to keep the creatures of the imagination
your creatures
and not turn them into our monsters.
And remember that sometimes monsters
only need to be kissed
to be turned into beautiful princes and princesses.

Thank you, God, for water,
for the water of the ocean
in which I paddle with my bare feet
and let the sand squish through my toes.
Thank you for the water from the brook
which flows even in the winter
under the ice.
Thank you for the water
in my bath in which I play
until I am clean.
Thank you for the water which I drink—
your water, clean and refreshing.
Help us care for your water, Lord,
and keep it as you made it
beautiful and clean.

I'm alone with my doll,
so I make believe.
I make believe I'm a mother.
Mothers are lots of things—
doctors, writers, lawyers, gardeners,
actresses, cooks, police officers,
sometimes even truck drivers.
And mothers.
Thank you, Lord.

Grandfather took us out
long after dark
and set his telescope up on the lawn
and showed us how to look through the lens.
We saw the mountains of the moon!
We saw the rings around Saturn!
We saw the stars in the Milky Way—
too many to count!
"See," Grandfather said,
"what wonders God has made!"
And then he hugged each one of us
and said, "And you are wondrous, too!"

Good night.
Good night daylight
and playing trains;
good night books,
and bread and butter
and games of make believe,
and brothers and sisters
and father and mother.
Good night, God.
Take care of us while we sleep,
and you have a good night, too.
Amen.